Archway Publishing books may be ordered through booksellers or by contacting:

Archway Publishing
1663 Liberty Drive
Bloomington, IN 47403
www.archwaypublishing.com
1-(888)-242-5904

ISBN: 978-1-4808-0823-2 (sc)
ISBN: 978-1-4808-0824-9 (e)

Library of Congress Control Number: 2014910060

Printed in the United States of America.

Archway Publishing rev. date: 06/06/2014

ENTHUSIASM EVERY DAY

ENTHUSIASM EVERY DAY

PICK YOURSELF UP AND ATTACK YOUR DAY WITH ENTHUSIASM

MARK D. GLEASON

Biography

Mark D. Gleason grew up in a small town in West Michigan. His business career began at a very young age. He started negotiations on the playground and sold everything from grape suckers to garden snakes. As he grew older, his interest in sales increased and the items he sold evolved into condominiums, subdivisions, and land developments. The son of a homebuilder, home sales came second nature to Mark. He found his passion in serving others and eventually discovered his niche in helping families find their new home. Mark's thirty-plus years of experience as a REALTOR span from owning his own real estate agency to managing various different companies.

Today, at the age of fifty-two, he still calls the same small town "home" and is always on the go, listing and selling properties. In his free time, Mark can be found hiking the sand dunes with his wife and business partner, Kim, or perch and bluegill fishing on Lake Michigan. More recently, Mark has coupled his sales experience with his ability to achieve through different speaking engagements. In doing what he does best – spreading knowledge with enthusiasm - he has gained much praise from those he has uplifted.

Acknowledgements

I wish to say THANK YOU to the following people for their help, love, support and guidance on this project:

My wife Kim Louise and our three daughters, Katy Louise, Kelsey Louise, and Kali Louise for your daily encouragement, inspiration, advice, intuition and love.

My mom and dad, Donald and Betty Gleason, and my in-laws, Jerry and Susan VanderMolen, for your faith in me and for keeping the lights on, which shows your unconditional support.

Many mentors along the way – without their help, this work wouldn't have come to paper.

My friends who've stood by me in good and bad times all deserve a big hug and a thank you.

My brothers and my sister, who all taught me the hard way.

To the thousands of clients, customers, and suppliers who attended to our needs, bought and sold, and came to our seminars and helped us tell our stories.

You have all helped show me the way, the truth, and wisdom. And to all those I didn't mention, thank you for supporting me in a lifetime of Enthusiasm Every Day!

Are *you* searching out wisdom? If yes, it's searching for you as well. Today and every day forward will become what you decide to make it. Are you ready for your daily dose of energy?

Your interests, desires, and abilities are energized by whatever fans your flame. Wisdom, energy, and enthusiasm deliver your destiny. You've studied the greats. Results are bound to follow you. Dynamic outcomes are your companions as you travel light and move swiftly across space. Somewhere within you, intrigue and nature balance and your talents collide as you are in your own element, learning from those who've come before you.

As you examine your life, questions manifest as experience in a passionate pursuit of knowledge. You have told yourself aloud hundreds of times, "I'm the passionate professional," never losing confidence and always in search of opportunity. All the spirits living among us cannot stop your optimism and experience and knowledge and wisdom that you so enjoy.

I'm excited to have you join me as I offer an optimistic outlook on life, business, love, happiness, motivation, and energy. The goal is that you emerge with a lifelong love for enthusiasm. The wisdom of learning new and exciting energy-filled knowledge will lead you on the path to your own life's destiny.

Read everyday for *enthusiasm; every day.*

January

January 1.   You Are

Think what you are;

(As some even say),

You are what you *think*, either way.

It might be best to say, "It's okay to get better each day!"

January 2.   Promises Kept

A New Year's increase,

Love life and keep spreading hugs and help.

You can do this; it's

One affirmation per day,

A delivery of inspiration and gratitude

For everyone to enjoy.

Bring it.

January 3.   Life's Prescription Is Balance

Finding a balance between work and relaxation

Is best described using the European principle.

(Americans appear to live to work,

while Europeans appear to work to live.)

If you've lost a job—work is living—

It's more like this.

It becomes a labor of love, having that job …

January 4.   *Use* or *Abuse*

A friend told us years ago,

"You can do nothing and get nothing."

It's called life's treatment formula for remaining the same.

A classic dilemma: 'Right' still appears to be 'right', right?

And wrong is *never* 'right'.

But for those who choose not to follow those rules, my

suggestion is to improve instead.

January 5.   Intelligence

Harboring ill will and holding onto

Unforgiveness clarifies your

Character.

Does nothing to the other;

Does everything to *you*.

Let go of the past and stop threatening your own intelligence.

By holding onto your grudges, you're holding your own

  success hostage.

January 6.   Think about It

What you dwell

On

Doesn't become your reality.

It

Becomes your fate.

You go as far as you can go, and you go on from there.

January 7.   On Course

You may only be a little off.

So do what works; don't do what doesn't work.

Make a difference.

It's called:

To change, you always have to

Rearrange, but to make a difference,

You've got to go the distance.

January 8.   Dream Big

If *you*

Want more, ask for it,

Want wealth, work for it.

Want happiness, go for it.

Whatever *you* want more of,

You've got to

Ask for it,

Work for it, and

Go for it.

January 9.   Ask, Believe, Receive

For *you* to become like the

change you see in others,

Don't expect *them* to change.

Only you can make that change—that change you wish

   to see in others.

January 10.   People of Success

They seem to listen successfully.

They practice their listening skills, which leads them to

   learning

And to action.

They know they can't beat the system; they give *no*

Cheap answers.

They know what you can't measure,

What you can't manage.

Do *you*?

January 11.   Close Networking

Money's the echo of success;

It networks closely with authenticity.

It sits close by its cousin, Value,

Who's near and dear to its father, Increase, and

Its mother, Compensation.

January 12.   Your Ability

I believe in you; now it's time you believe in *you*.

Your success depends on your own ability to believe in
   yourself.

January 13.   The Speed of Right

Funny, while the truth is still trying to tie its shoelaces,

Wrong information travels all the way around the world.

January 14.   Set Sail Cautiously

Dad always said, "The only ship guaranteed to sink is a
partnership."

Not sure if that's 100 percent for sure, but if you've
experienced a bad partnership, you can see how it just
might hold water.

Some ground rules for establishing one that hopefully
floats.

1)   Have written rules, a manual while at sea.
2)   Stick by the rule in the roughest of waters.
3)   Be fair; everyone in the boat must row equally.
4)   Make sure the plan's original objective is seaworthy.
5)   If heavy winds come upon someone's boat, help
     everyone to shore quickly.
6)   No partner is an island or can be expected to do it all.

After reviewing these rules, maybe you should consider
A short cruise instead of
A long, seasick journey.

January 15. Life's Vending Machine

There's no vending machine offering success.

The only real option is the *change* machine.

January 16. Close It Up

Man's

Greatest

Lies

Happen

When

His

Mouth

Opens.

January 17. I Know Nothing

Just about the moment we realize we really have figured

it out,

That's the moment we know *nothing* but realize everything.

January 18.   You Can Rise

Rise today toward riches.

Or

Cave toward caution.

If you think you can,

more than likely you can.

Think about success

Or

Worry about failure.

How you think determines what you will become.

January 19.   Personal Treatment

I'm a *patient* person.

But too much waiting and I lose my patience.

Then I end up at the hospital being the patient.

January 20.   Never Money, Never

Money was never a big motivator,

Unless I had none.

January 21.   Half the Battle

Learning *how* is half of making it happen; the other half is

   a big yoo-hoo!

You heard it right –

It's you.

There's no mistaken danger in trying, for it is guaranteed

   failure if you don't.

January 22.   Overboard

Overcaution isn't an approach or a way to head out into

   the world.

Approach today thinking about life like this: I'm throwing

   all caution to the

Wind.

If you think you're wealthy

You're 90 percent there.

If you think you're poor

You're 100 percent there.

And that's just unfair.

January 23.   Paths

The final road

Of

Success

Is

The long hard road

Of

Failure.

1 percent of life's successes come from 99 percent of life's
    failures.

Get yourself past life's successes—

Barriers also known as the *fear of failure*.

January 24.   Big Book

Some people's ignorance can't be described in the

encyclopedia.

The book's not large enough to hold it all.

You can make some of the people happy some of the

time, but not all the people all the time, unless

You have a higher calling.

January 25.   Up and Away

When climbing the mountains they call life, or dealing in

real estate,

You

Have to go

Back down

Before you

Can climb

Higher.

January 26.   It's Complicated.

Leading a complicated life?

Let others live without your complications.

Maintaining their complicated lives is how they avoid
   change.

Worry less about what people think and life becomes less
   complicated.

January 27.   Who Gives Up

People give up and

Some begin again.

Some people think they need a facelift,

When *all* they probably require is a nonsurgical mind-lift,

Or what's known as a mental, reconstructive makeover.

Never give up; just try your very best to start over.

January 28.　Discoveries

You'll

Find

What

You're

Focusing

On.

Proper questions bring proper answers. Never stop
asking them.

January 29.　Trouble Clef

Take *note*:

Those who never laugh,

Miss out

On the world's

Best

Music.

Laughter—sweet soul music.

January 30.   *Age*

Do you

Act

Your age?

Let's hope

Not.

Evaluate where you are now.

Thinking young and acting the same

Will

Keep

You young!

January 31.   Glasses On

We *see* some people

In our lives

With whom

We

Struggle

To

Really see

Eye-to-eye.

The cure isn't to change eyeglasses.

Best way to look at this is to put certain people in your

   blind spot.

February

February 1.   Commissions

It's

Not

What

We

Charge,

It's

What

We

Earn.

To succeed in life, everyone should be on commission compensation, at least once.

February 2.   Don't Lose It

How you see the world changes *nothing*,

If you don't change how you see the world.

February 3.   Time Management

Wealthy people

Seldom say good-bye during their phone conversations.

Why? Poor social skills or time management principles?

Don't waste time on what doesn't matter, because what
    doesn't matter can be a waste of time.

February 4.   Your Future

The future belongs to you if you are willing to constantly
    move forward with
Relentless motion and a steadfast commitment to do
    what is right.

February 5.   Listened to Something Funny

Listening leads to
Laughter.

Lighten up,

Loosen up,

Let up,

Live it up.

Let's all head to da U.P.

Understandable if you live it up in Michigan. Laugh if

off …

February 6.   Control Anger

Why control anger?

Just *not* gonna

Let it ruin

My day.

Something better is

Gonna be

Coming my way.

I know—easy to say, aye.

Don't get mad, make yourself glad.

February 7.   Know It

What you

Don't know

Really can

Hurt you.

Read to succeed, but maybe you already know that.

Pick up a book and take a good look.

February 8.   Family and Happiness

Two (2)

Important branches

To hang

Onto

While

You're climbing

The

Tree

They

Call success.   Family and Happiness.

February 9.   Step UP

What people learn

Most

From

Defeat:

They learned they

Needed

To get

Back up on

Their

Feet.

February 10.   New Research Reveals

From a highly accredited research group came these
incredible survey results:

Three out of three

People

Agree,

Two

Is

Better

Than

One

A second opinion

Can't hurt.

February 11.   Good Manners

Excuse me—

Excuses are for people who haven't really got one.

It is always best to excuse yourself, but it is not something

   you can expect someone else to handle for you.

February 12.   Friendships

A

Really

Good

Friend

Makes

His or her

Friend

Feel

Really

Good.

February 13.   Growing It

Plants are like people,

Nothing grows fast when

Dirt keeps getting thrown on them.

February 14.   Time's a Wasting

Do not waste time on your problems,

All you can do is prolong them, anyhow.

February 15. Insecurities Road Race

If what you are running toward is security,

Then what you are running from is usually insecurity.

February 16. What Works

People can ignore what works,

But eventually what works

Can't be ignored.

Don't ignore it; you can do it.

February 17. Limits

Only you

Put limits

On the life

You live.

February 18.   Success in Business

Being a success in business is about being personal,

   sincere, and treating people kindly.

Simple.

February 19.   Dream Big

There is no excuse necessary for accomplishment.

February 20.   What You Think About

What you dwell on doesn't become your destiny,

It becomes your fate.

February 21.   Increase Formula

Increase income by more than 400 percent.

Read, write, and study.

Learn to communicate.

Make small incremental upgrades to yourself.

Become a better you, and you sincerely become better.

February 22.   Say It

It's what you don't say now that's going to matter later.

Pick up the phone, text it, tweet it, or Skype it.

Just don't delay—life's short.

February 23.   Wisdom's Gift

A lifetime journey

To assemble wisdom's success clues,

Finding those patterns and habits.

The success of today is a gift from yesterday's hard work.

Hard work uncovers clues to your own patterns, which

follow your daily movements that can possibly become

your life's rituals.

Whoever you've decided to be, that's who *we* all want to see.

February 24. How You See

It matters little how others *see you*.

Really what matters most is how *you see* yourself.

February 25. Pass It On

Sharing is the same as caring,

So keep passing it along.

There are lots of people who care for you. If you think no

one else does, well, you are wrong because

I care about you.

February 26. Respect

People who do not respect you have no respect for

themselves.

February 27.   Future Fixes

A

Person

Can't

Fix

The

Future

Without

Being

Genuinely

Sincere

About

The

Past.

February 28.   Introspective

You must first be sold on yourself
Before a long-term relationship of selling can occur—
Mainly by telling yourself that you can sell yourself.

Same occurs with life; one must love him or herself
   before that person can truly love another.

March

March 1.   Cut It Short

Rarely are there short-term solutions to long-term
   problems,
Unless everyone pulls together.

If you're not pulling together, you'll be pulling apart.

March 2.   Music for Life

Listening to music is the universal law of expression;
   some even love to make it.
At times, we choose to listen to our own soul's sounds.
They can heal just about anything.

March 3.   Are You?

It's your choice.

Let no one else decide if you are happy.

Happiness is up to you and only you.

March 4.   Your First Worry

Ninety-nine percent of what we worry, doubt, fear, fret,

and stew about *never* actually happens.

Simple solution: don't worry.

Worrying won't change the outcome.

March 5.   The Future—It's Yours.

We all have one—

A future.

Be fearless,

Optimistic,

Positively enthusiastic about life.

Just keep rolling in the right direction.

It's your future—no one else can say that.

Let no one else decide it for you.

March 6.   Everyone Thinks They've Got the Answer

Simply offering situations without *solutions* is like trying
   to ride a bike without a chain;
It'll get you nowhere.
It's like offering a diagnosis without being curious about
   the cause.

March 7.   Time to Release

Letting go is proof
You are stronger than you think.

Holding on is also proof, at times, of just how weak we
   can be.

March 8.　Expensive Reading Material

Anyone can avoid messages in books by not reading
　them,
But what's the cost to you if you choose not to
Read them?

There's really no excuse; there are books on tapes or CDs.

March 9.　What You See

What you see when you look outside yourself is exactly
　what's staring you in the face—
Reality.

March 10.　By the Horns

When indecision has run out
And
Determination has run in,
Improvements and achievements arrive.

March 11.   Learning

Learning to read is

More about reading to learn.

March 12.   Never, Never, Never

There's really enough for now.

Some people only care about themselves and

Not enough about the detail.

And that's enough for now.

March 13.   Who's Excited?

Enthusiasm

Outlives

All

Numbers.

Some call this a birthday.

They say you are only as old as you feel.

Someone replied with, "I feel like I am young again."

March 14.   How Do You See You?

You have got to *manage* yourself,

Before

You can *imagine* yourself.

How you see you, is a thousand times more important

than how anyone else sees you.

Can you see that?

March 15.   Dad's Memo

It takes no longer to do it right the first time.

So why are people's habits the opposite?

Actually, if you follow instructions and do it right the first

time, you save time in the long run.

March 16.   Critics

Everyone knows the critic, the ones with the critical eyes.

Compliments or criticisms, eyes for success—

That's not a critic to me.

Are you the critic or just a critical thinker?

Whatever you may be, let others see you, as you want to
be seen.

Mr. Nice or Mr. Nasty—either way it is okay with me.

March 17.   Start to Finish

When you plan to finish what *you* start,

It's important that you start what *you* planned.

Get started today, and never leave it, until you finish it
your way.

March 18.   Real or Magic

There's no magic trick; it's more about the human eye.

Don't be fooled by another guy; real magic is a miracle of
the eye.

Experiencing faith through birth is about loving your guy.

That's not a magic trick.

March 19.   Mom's Mottos

- Cover your mouth when you cough.
- Be on time.
- Do it, ditch it, or delete it.
- Help those in need.
- Save more than you spend.
- Practice, practice, practice.
- Make your own bed.
- Go to church.
- Turn off the lights when you leave a room.
- No closing occurs till we leave the bank.
- Be fair.
- Chew your food well.
- Experience is the greatest teacher.
- Wait for others to be served.
- Wash your hands continually.
- Be a friendship maker.

- Help those who can't help themselves.

- Give accordingly.

March 20.   Your head

No one knows what's in your head,

What you're taking about,

Feeling, hearing, or smelling.

Your thoughts are yours,

Sometimes what's in your head is better left unsaid.

Guess that's where the saying came from—

If you haven't got anything good to say, then say
   nothing.

March 21.   The Problems

Unless you take on everyone else's problems of the day,

You will not be a part of their problem today.

March 22. Want or Not

Want is not bad,

Not to want is not bad either.

People who want everything but do nothing—

What they soon discover is that more for less is delivering

   much less than more.

March 23. Down or Up

Arrogance

Or

Ignorance,

Two parts

Of

Success

And

Failure.

March 24.   Discoveries

Success in life

Revolves around

Two important

Characteristics:

Fear and failure.

When you lose both, you find success.

At times, it is important to lose something to really find
what you are looking for.

March 25.   Habits Have It

Developing a successful habit may just be doing
something slightly different
Than anyone else is,
And doing it well.

March 26. Cost vs. Value

Why is it that some people seem to know the cost of
   everything,
But the value of nothing?

And most let you know it all too well.

March 27. Work, Work, Work

No matter who you work for, your main employer is *you*.
The self-employed employee, *you*.

No one can expect more from you than you do.
Do you?

March 28. Logic Would Say

Ignore *all* the logic of those screaming at you,
"It absolutely won't work."
Trust that one reason why it will—*you*.

So many people today hammer away at what you do,

Letting you know if you do it their way, it might work,

But any other way is not in the cards.

Wrong—

They don't know you, do they?

March 29. Overdoing It

Try not to overanalyze or overcomplicate life.

Be fast on your feet.

Be ready to move over and over,

Till you need to move again.

Repeating the same behaviors will just deliver similar results.

So adapt or become obsolete.

March 30. Sweet-Tasting Juice

Today's principles for continued success:

After you have made lemonade from all the lemons available,

You have got to keep planting those little lemon seeds.

March 31.   Use your Senses

Turning sales whine into fine wine.

"If your message isn't captivating, it's not your prospect's
 fault."

What you say can't be taken back, but if said just right,
 why would you need to?

April

April 1.   A Silent Speech

Leave them speechless—that is really saying something.
Silence, most times, has the loudest impact from the
person telling his true-life story.

If only he kept quiet about it.

April 2.   Excuses

A lack of knowledge cannot be found on anyone's excuse
list. Accomplishing greatness has no
List of excuses.

April 3.   A Piece of Mind

Peace of mind does come in a can.
"I can" is found when you stop saying "I can't."

April 4.   Dinner is on

It's accep*table* to be profi*table*; it comes from being
accoun*table*.

It's not always predic*table*, but if you work hard it is
inevi*table*.

Being chari*table*, exci*table*, marke*table*, hospi*table*,
adap*table*, and trus*table* almost always assures

One outcome—

Being s*table*,

And it comes from sitting together at your family *table*.

April 5.   Read On

People who refuse to read what is right will eventually
find themselves being left.

April 6. Who's Counting?

No one person has got more or less time than 24/7, 365
    days per year.
Now what we do with that time—
Well it's amazing how we make time for what we want.

And how there's always too much time for what we don't.

April 7. Believing in *You*

You can make anything happen; just believe in yourself.

April 8. On Strike

People who've made demands for increased pay
    eventually end up without.
Nagging for more money means doing nothing, and that
    won't work.

Solution: make yourself invaluable.

April 9.   Finding Firm Ground

Blaming yourself for your own unhappiness and
   self-doubt
Is no foundation to stand on.

April 10.   *You* Already Have It

When you stop checking your bank's balance
And start checking your life's balance,
What do *you* find?

Real-life balance.

April 11.   Wrong or Right

Being with someone who treats you wrong,
Can't be right.

Treating everyone like you want to be treated—that's a
   treat.

April 12.   Never Accept Defeat

Those who can admit temporary defeat,

Prove they'll *never* be beat.

It's *okay* to have temporary setbacks and failures along

the way; they are nothing more than

Life's lessons strengthening you.

April 13.   Thoughts

Our thoughts control our lives.

Let *no* one else's control yours.

April 14.   All *Wet*

A child wishing to remain dry must never go near water.

An adult, who can't stay dry, must be all wet.

April 15.   Bottom-Feeders

When you have been on the bottom,

To understand what it means to be at the top means you

  know what it takes to be in to both places.

April 16.   Play Fair

In this life and

As Douglas MacArthur said,

"You will be remembered for the rules you break."

We say,

"Better yet, you will be best remembered for the rules

  you helped to make."

April 17.   You Are the Best

If you can't give it your best, then give it a rest.

For without your best, it's hard to obtain success.

Failure isn't final; defeat doesn't mean you're beat.

Three little words:

I won't quit.

April 18.   Thank You, Thank You

It's not about you, the *thank you*.

It's about *them*; say *thank you*.

It's a good thing, that *thank you*.

It's understood, that thing, that *thank you*.

It's for you to hear, that *thank you*.

It's not about you, that *thank you*.

It's two small words, *thank you*.

Its results are immeasurable.

It's not a thing you can get a refund on, that *thank you*.

It's short and sweet.

It's thank you time—thank *you*.

April 19.   A Pet's Policy

I've learned a lot about people by listening to my dog.

Most times, dogs make more sense.

April 20.   A Quiet Speech

When it's time to give your life's great acceptance speech,

use no words.

April 21.   A Big Thank You

Thank goodness one size doesn't fit all.

What fits for you, gives me fits.

Stop squeezing into what doesn't really fit –

You?

April 22.   An Opinion

Everyone's got one and most people are always sharing it

with the world.

You might be saying, "An opinion, right?"

Maybe it would make more sense if every day we could

all share *only* one bit of advice.

According to leading psychologists, IQ accounts for just

20 percent of success:

EQ (emotional quotient) is actually where it's at.

Motivation, empathy, and social skills are the other 80

percent to work on.

Today, get motivated and socialize and fire up.

It's part of your IQ.

April 23.   Shush Up

Never say the words "I can't" ever again.

By removing these words,

New doors of opportunity will begin to open

automatically for you.

A friend asked the other day how to continue to be a huge success?

One word, *enthusiasm*!

April 24.   The Time Is Here

Don't be discouraged; become encouraged.

Do outwardly nice things today; the world will appreciate it.

Do the right thing, even if the wrong thing seems to be everywhere.

April 25.   Good Food

Never eat in a restaurant with *no* lines,

And one, large menu.

April 26. Right or Wrong

Right is what

We are faced with

When wrong is all that is

Left.

April 27. Feeling Disorganized

Simple Fix.

Get organized.

Some people don't because they won't, and that's the
    end of that.

April 28. Consideration

Things wrong in your own world?

Is it possible it's you?

People's problems probably persist, preoccupying
    passion, pleasure, and pain.

April 29.   Rekindle

When your fire goes out,

It's simple—

Build a new one.

You can relight any person's candle,

But first you must not let your own flame die out.

April 30.   Roadblocks

Lose your *obstacles*.

Break those *habits*.

Take on those *challenges*.

Tackle those *dilemmas*.

Overcome your *fears*.

Stop all *doubt*.

No more *worries*.

Consider it like this…

Your roadblocks are to be left *behind*.

May

May 1.   A Lawyer's Stories

Where there's a will, there's a way. Where is that place?

   Oh, maybe an estate lawyer wrote it.

Maybe it means if you have will power, you can

   accomplish or become accomplished.

Some just want to do it their own way.

Where is this place, where you can accomplish "a way"?

Maybe it's just along life's way.

May 2.   Expectations

Never expect what others expect.

Instead, expect only what you'd expect from yourself.

May 3. Words That Listen

Want to sell more?

Say less; you can't fake being the quiet one.

Your clients and customers always get the first, middle,

    and last words.

Listen up.

With that, you get

"The *sale*."

May 4. It's on the Way—Help!

A strong person helps the weak.

That, in turn, allows the weak to help the strong.

It's the circle of life.

May 5.   I-Am-Possible Thinking

(ITYS) = *I told you so*. Know-it-all types.

Problem arises when they tell you before,

And remind you after,

Everything that happens in life.

Hey, some things in life people need to figure out for

themselves.

Everything is possible; nothing is impossible.

Here's the proof:

You.

You are living proof that anything is possible.

Now say this out loud, "I'm possible."

You can accomplish anything.

Okay.

Listen to everyone, except those who say you can't do it.

May 6.   Inside of Words

One man said to another, "You're probably not going to

 be*lie*ve this but—"

Right then, the fella's listening stopped

Because

He knew that what he would hear next was probably

 a *lie*.

May 7.   Right *Now*

Those who live for this very moment, this second, *really*

 live.

May 8.   Duck Soup

One thing a person should do every day:

You'll never be negatively criticized for telling someone

 something positive.

It's as easy as duck soup.

May 9.   Oh, No One

*Depend*ing on yourself—that's *happiness*.

Depend on no one—that allows great in*depend*ence.

May 10.   Daily Recipe

Everyone has at least one recipe. Do *you*?

Add a wee bit of each of these to yours:

1) Success

2) Dress

3) Cleaning up the mess

4) Less stress

5) Cleanliness

6) Confessions

7) Tastefulness

8) Obsessions

9) Happiness

10) Kindness

May 11.   Indefensible

When apologies appear prior to accusations being made,
Admissions of the crime may have just happened.

When we listen closely to what people are telling us, it's
   easy to figure out
What's about to happen.

May 12.   Looking Back

When people take a closer look at *you*,
What they see should make them *happy* too.

May 13.   Kick Back

Those who repeatedly kick others eventually become
   known as heels.

May 14.   What Is for Sure

Uncertainty is *new, unique.*

Shut up about it.

Instead get productively busy,

Because that's where it's at.

May 15.   Is It Struggle or Defeat?

Never give up,

Never give in.

Fight like hell

And forgive again.

Everyone is wrestling with something, no matter who
they are.

Defeat isn't fatal, unless you allow it to become final.

You can overcome anything by doing this:

Don't let whatever you may be struggling with keep you
down.

Simply put, keep those feet moving and lose the frown.

May 16. *Change* We *Try*

If you can't inspire people, then by all means, get out of
the way.

May 17. Optional

Two options:

Perpetuate more false hope

Or bring dreams in check.

Maybe you think you've tried everything.

For some people, failure isn't an option.

Success is as simple as sunlight. Keep on searching for the
light.

May 18. Pipe Down

The listener is always the learner.

No one gains knowledge with one's own mouth open.

May 19. Woulda, Coulda, Shoulda

It is one thing to woulda, coulda, shoulda all over
yourself.

It is a whole other thing for someone else to woulda,
coulda, shoulda all over you.

The moral of the story is
Keep criticism to yourself, the person who more than
likely needs it *most*.
All you need is love.

May 20. Incompleted Actions

Never leave your actions incomplete when you are
speaking your true feelings with a friend.

May 21. Deception

Have *great* faith in friends—
At least until they don't deserve it.

May 22. Keep Trying It

Practice.

It's what's practical,

If you want to succeed, that is.

May 23. Controlled Hearing

Whatever people tell you about you has nothing to do
with how you feel about you.

It has everything to do with how they feel about
themselves.

Control what you hear, not what they say.

May 24. *Now* Prove It

Just because people hear themselves and discuss
themselves,

Doesn't prove they're experts themselves.

May 25.   Those Who Are Uncomfortable

The only people who take comfort in being

uncomfortable

Are those who are satisfied being uncomfortable.

To achieve greatness, one must be uncomfortable.

Some people, however, take comfort in you being

Uncomfortable.

May 26.   Walk Through It

The only failure known to man is not having tried when

the doors of opportunity opened.

May 27.   It Itches

A good idea is the same as a good back scratcher—

One scratches your back and one scratches lots of others'

backs.

May 28. To Stand for

Someone said, "If you stand for nothing, you'll fall for

everything."

Not you, right?

In this crazy world we should run from making

judgments

And toward taking responsibility,

Which allows us to

Stand up for what we think is right.

Do you stand for the other guy, or just for yourself?

A tough question with today's battles is "The Law to

Witness,"

Also known as, "To stand for someone other than

yourself."

Do you?

May 29. To Keep or Not

We have a friend who *saves* it all,

Boxes and stuff and bags of it all.

What for?

He can't take it with him—all.

What is he storing it for?

Is he a gatherer or hoarder of all?

Is this your art? Cluttering up your life, saving it all,

Items nobody wants but you?

Seems kind of compulsive.

This is your time to become an "un-hoarder" of it all.

May 30. "Ancient Gleason Secret"

Work hard—make a living.

Work hard on oneself—make a fortune.

May 31. Be Careful

If you can't be kind, then you'd better be careful.

June

June 1.   Life's View

Past performance holds *no* promise of future success.

But in life, what else do we believe?

It's how we are seen by others, based on our past actions,
deeds, and behaviors.

That's why they call it our *past*.

How do you want others to view you and your past?

Maybe start fresh today and do something good for
another human being.

Leave the place, as they say, better than you found it.

That's life's view—

At the least leave the place for others to see it their way.

June 2.   *Stop* Collecting

Peace.

Peace cannot truly be found by simply collecting pieces.

How do we appraise a great attitude?

Its value is priceless.

June 3.   The Pirate's Patch

The law of knowing what to overlook -

Failing to notice a technique crafted by perceptive

   people.

June 4.   The Rung of Success

Climb

Enough

Of

The

Right

Ladders,

And

Doors

Will

Open.

June 5.   Free Reports

Free reports reveal information someone else couldn't
   sell.

Normally you get what you pay for. Free can be
   worthless.

June 6.   Who's Holding *You* Back?

Only

You

Put

Limits

On

Life.

June 7.   Addictive Failure

Failure is life's best teacher.

Acknowledge your guilt and turn that acknowledgment into

A productive emotion.

Only you can leave the inside of failure.

It's important to admit in order to embrace.

Get accustomed to failure; it's an important ingredient

that is

Present prior to success.

June 8.   Conversations with Yourself

Listen to yourself.

You are your own biggest advocate.

Heal with humor and the help of yourself.

Of the 57,000 conversations we enjoy within ourselves

daily, just who else do you really expect to

Listen to?

You can heal yourself by listening to yourself.

Listen up.

June 9. Help

A strong person helps the weak,

Which allows the weak to help the strong.

It's called what goes around comes around.

Good always is *good*.

June 10. I Love You

Love isn't the *greatest* of all gifts.

The giving of it—that's where *love's* at.

June 11. Acknowledgement

We

Begin

To

Understand

Everything

When

We

Acknowledge

That

We

Don't

Know

Everything.

It's called balanced perspective.

June 12.   Never *Too* Late

One thing a person should do every day:

Tell someone something nice.

So today,

It's not too late to let it out.

You are a great person. Start with that.

June 13.   Those Who Think

The technology of today relieves men and women of

   their ability to think,

But what's in question is

Whether or not the majority of people ever did think.

June 14.   Fill Her Up

Acceptance:

It's the fuel in life's gas tank.

It drives you past

Where you presently are,

On to where you're

Supposed to be.

Accept where you are today,

Do the same with where everyone else is at.

June 15.   Reminder

Note to *self*:

Keep up the *good* work.

Sincerely,

Self.

June 16.   Careful Now

Thinking about what you say

And saying what you think

Can get you in trouble,

Or keep you from it.

June 17.   Want To

If you really want to figure out how to become worth

   more in the world,

Learn to ask better questions.

Your income is in direct proportion to the quality of the

   questions you ask.

June 18.   Figure It Out

Figuring out the rules of the game is more than half the

   battle.

Now just figure out how to improve

Upon your own game.

That's more than the other half of the battle.

June 19.   It's *You*

Being alive is proof

Anything can be fixed.

June 20.   *Fearless* Checklist

Lose all doubt.

Stop denying it.

Become brave.

Take risks.

Eliminate worry.

Plunge.

Block concerns.

See possibilities.

How others see you has nothing to do with overcoming

your fears.

Don't be afraid to face them,

Your fears,

Face them head on.

June 21.   A Crack in the Door

If you want happiness to truly get inside, you must

Leave the door of *enthusiasm* open.

June 22.   Responsibility Today

Lose the words and deeds associated with '*If*'.

Replace with '*when*'.

Try this unique Principle of *When*:

Don't make it a promise, but make it a destiny.

Be the person the world knows will be able to deliver.

Takes time, but the rewards will be many—mainly
    respect, friendship, and confidence.
Sincere responsibility for today delivers the *when* of
    tomorrow,
Bury all the *'ifs'* today.

June 23.   Hungry?

Need more business? Feeling hungry?
What you need is to give yourself a good, old-fashioned
    knuckle sandwich.
Maybe you just need to put your fist down upon yourself.

June 24.   My Friend

He taught me
To gather knowledge.
He taught me how to use it.
He taught me how to continue on with it.
He taught me how not to abuse it.

What did I learn?

Share it and pass it along.

What did my friend's wisdom teach me most?

True friendships deserve a sincere thank you.

June 25.   Give Everyone Time

An old banner hangs on the wall.

It says, "Return all calls within twenty-four hours."

Father-in-law says, "Ignore them long enough, they go
away."

Not sure I like either…

Better saying might be,

"Be courteous with time and follow up."

Your time is important, so is everyone else's.

So just simply be friendly and give everyone time.

June 26.   An Ear Organ Donor

Lots of ways to give of yourself.

That's a good way to donate.

Too many people give away too much of their vocal

 organs.

It can be noisy.

Don't talk about yourself. Only *you* really want to or enjoy

 hearing it anyway.

Use your vocal organs less, be an ear donor.

Good things happen when you become an ear donor.

 Listen.

June 27.   Don't Lose Hope

Losing hope for tomorrow ensures another hopeless

 today.

June 28.   The Marketing Sea

Don't get lost in the marketing sea.

Can't control callous clients, crowds, or costs.

Have to navigate a clear path toward success.

It appears that might be how to find it.

One row, one bite.

June 29.   A Ruler for Measurement

When measurement is involved,

Growth and expansion appear.

When you lift the limits of your thinking,

You expand the limits of your life.

Think and act big.

June 30. *What* Do We *See*

When you see one door shut and two new ones open,

It's confusing.

But the issue is whether or not you even see the two

   open doors,

Being so focused on why the

One door shut.

July

July 1.   The *Universe*

Those who grasp the *all of the universe*

Live in a place called *delusion*.

July 2.   Prep

Those who prepare for little

Find exactly what they've prepared for.

July 3.   Deciphering

A vehicle pulls up behind you at a stoplight.

You look at it in your mirror.

E C N A L U B M A.

Had you read this by actually turning your head and

    seeing what was right there,

You would have been able to decipher the correct word
   formations.
How do we see life?
Sometimes we are simply looking at life backward,
Through a rear-view mirror.
Perspective,
Your mirror can cause you to see things backward.
Some things, as they appear, are momentarily reversed.

July 4.   Keep Climbing

"Always keep your feet moving."
–Chuck Basset

As you struggle to try to get yourself on the stairway of
   accomplishment,
Make sure of your direction.
Are you going up or heading down?

July 5.   Snowman or a *No Man*

Not too many people advance in their professions today

by saying,

"It can't be done."

It can get cold being a *no man*.

July 6.   Stop

A few individuals just might educate themselves through

examination of their own problems,

If by chance they weren't so occupied by self-contradiction.

The best advice you can give yourself is that today,

Every day,

You are always improving.

July 7.   Keep Talking

Many people *talk* to themselves.

Those who don't must be questioned.

For goodness sake, it's part of the

Thinking process.

The learning part occurs with

The listening process.

Have you heard yourself lately?

Listen up.

July 8.   The Pretender

When your body is in rejection,

What you've been experiencing is

The act of pretending everything is all right.

Listen to your body; it's never wrong.

July 9.   Excited

Accomplishments with extraordinary results must have

enormous

Enthusiasm.

Get fired up to deliver your plan.

July 10.   Knowledge

True knowledge isn't something you imagine,

It's something you acquire.

July 11.   Everyone Tells You Something

Stop believing everything everyone tells you.

Just because people tell you what you want to hear,

That doesn't mean what you want to hear is true.

July 12.   Ahead of Times

What is before us is far more important than what is
    behind us.

July 13.   *Can You* Taste It?

Keep eating desserts.
Keep getting stressed.

Desserts spelled backward
Spells *stressed*.

Stop it.
You can almost taste it.
Can't you see it too?
That's backward thinking.

July 14.   Answers

The answer to the question,
We already know,
Is found within.

July 15.   Do You Hear It?

While listening to the voices in my head,

I've decided I need to become harder of hearing,

But sometimes the ideas I hear are insanely awesome.

Listen to yours, okay?

July 16.   Happy and Excited

Do whatever

Makes *you*

Smile!

July 17.   When Experience Matters

Education is cheap

Compared to the cost of

Experience.

July 18.   People *Wants*

Want what others don't have.

Do what they're *not* going to do!

July 19.   Accomplishments

Time can limit your thinking.

Do not let it limit your *life*.

People think time will go on forever; however, for people
who spend their time thinking time never Ends, well,
they have just limited themselves.

July 20.   The Great Ship, Waiting List

Lots of people live their lives aboard a ship called the
Waiting List,

Just waiting for this and that to happen.

A few figure out that waiting is a disease,

The symptoms of which are delay, frustration, and
indecision.

Don't delay; make a move, and do it today.

That's how you get off the Waiting List.

July 21.   No Reason

Trying to reason,

Unsuccessfully,

With an unreasonable person,

Proves there can be two people who can't reason it out,

Reinforcing that everyone is really good at his or her own

gross

Rationalizations of their personal, distorted reality.

July 22.   For *Dad*

The Builder's Creed—some know this as the verbal

apprentice lesson.

Dad always said, "We're not building houses, boys; we're

building character."

July 23. Shaking It

Dancing in the rain could create *a storm afoot*.

Dance till you can't.

July 24. Who Lives Where

Today the address for ignorance

Is easy to find.

July 25. The Goal Line

Making goals with no foreseeable end in sight is like

   screaming at yourself alone in the dark

And expecting someone else to

Answer.

July 26. Who's *Yours*

Being your own

Best friend

Allows you to

Tell 'em off

At anytime.

Go screw yourself.

I hear what

You're saying.

Don't agree,

But I'm

Listening.

July 27.   Those Reasons

Stop right where you are today and answer this:

Do you have what you want?

Or do you have a list loaded with reasons why you don't?

List of possible reasons why you're *not* successful.

1)   The interest rates

2)   The market

3)   Your boss

4)   Training

5) The rules

6) *No* one understands.

One item missing on the excuse list,

Probably the most important one,

You!

July 28. You're Not There Yet

Reaching the *end* of your rope.

Not there yet.

You haven't overdone it,

You've realized it before you're all tied up in knots.

July 29. Pete's Sake

If you don't believe in you,

For Pete's sake,

Why do you expect anyone else to?

July 30. Improvement

No one is forcing you to get better or improve.

They can't do it for you,

Anyway.

July 31. Verbal Make Up

It is good to give a compliment.

It feels good to receive one too.

Ask yourself: *Have I told another recently how important he*

or she is to me?

A simple showing of support can be amazing.

Both you and me.

August

August 1.   D - D - D - D - D

Delivering

Daily

Determination

Determines

Destiny.

You can't change your thoughts without changing the
   way you think.

August 2.   Garden of Eden

Don't waste another day trying to take a bite out of
   someone else's apple.
Grow your own.

August 3.   Life's Projections

If you are at a point in your life where *nothing* can get
    better, then read *no* further.
If that isn't *you*, then change is for *you*.

How to change:
Lots of hard work, most of it is sitting right in front of you.
Get up, project yourself forward, and become the change
    you want to see in you.

It is only being restricted by what's between your left
    and right ears.

August 4.   Full of LOVE

People who appear full of love don't really need to
    show it.
It's just that easy to see.
It's written all over them.

August 5.   Willingness

Why is it that people seem to want what they can't have,

Yet aren't willing to do what's necessary to have what

  they want?

August 6.   The Facts, Blurred

Try not to jumble the facts with commentary.

Keep records of what you have done,

Just in case someone asks.

August 7.   Speak *Up*

Don't expect anyone to come to your rescue

When you haven't let the world know you need rescuing.

August 8.   Reeducate

You've proven you're smart;

The problem is only one person knows it.

People can reeducate themselves once they admit they
  need to.

August 9.   Take Good Care

REPUTATION

Honesty, ethics, morals,

Commitment, trustworthiness, responsibility,

Fairness, compliance, standards.

Like a solid building has its proper foundation, planned
  to stand the test of time, so are individuals'

Foundations key to standing integrity's test of time.

Each word listed is key to a long prosperous life with
  honor and respect for all.

August 10.   Keep Swinging the Bat

As long as you keep playing, you are still in the game.

When you don't, you won't.

August 11.   They Do

Without questioning everything, some things get

   through.

Yes, they do.

It's nice to have someone in your corner,

Especially when your back's to the wall.

August 12.   Can't Happen

The *only* thing in life that cannot happen today

Is what you allow not to happen today.

Anything is possible,

Unless you keep it from happening.

August 13.   Do You See It?

The world and its people are beautiful

Beyond description.

Too bad so many people are blind to it.

August 14.   No Debts

Nothing.

It's what this whole wide world owes *you*.

Simple as that.

August 15.   Which Side Is *Yours*?

Their group

Or

Your group.

One accomplishes,

One claims they do.

Which is

Your

Group?

That's the

Group

For

You.

August 16.   Right or Wrong

I value your opinion;

It appears you don't value mine.

Either way, I know

I'm right

And you're wrong.

Guess that proves what an opinion is worth.

August 17.   Involvement

Most people choose not to get involved.

But when they want change,

They can't change the fact that they decided *not* to get

   involved.

August 18.   It Will Go Away

How can we fight the problems of the day?

Laugh it off until they go *away*!

August 19.   Doubting the Truth

The truth

Has no doubts

Especially when

It's not bent.

August 20.   Quit Bringing It Up

I remembered something from a long time ago that
  made me *very mad*,
Until I forgot it.

This is why our brains don't always remember things
  right away.
Some things are better left that way.

August 21.   Beginnings and Endings

He who refuses to take the first step assures himself of
  being stuck.

The absence of a beginning assures the absence of an

ending; at least in the race we call life.

Those who fail to start have already started to fail.

August 22.   They Come and They Go

Opportunities –

They're like ships passing in the night.

Make sure that yours don't sail away

Without you aboard them.

August 23.   Straighten Them *Out*

The facts can be *hard* to believe,

Because it's *hard* to believe the facts.

August 24.   *One* and *Only*

People who stay out of sight and out of mind

Also stay out of promotions.

August 25.   Give It Up

Three little words to remember

When you feel like throwing in the towel:

Never give up.

August 26.   Fools Sail Away

Truth and lies blend perfectly upon the tongues of two fools –

One who speaks and one who believes.

August 27.   For Richer or Poorer

If honesty leaves you rich,

Then dishonesty leaves you poor.

August 28.   What Is In It?

The office mission statement reads something like this:

You don't always have to speak when you are spoken to.

August 29. Life's Road Blocks

Obstacles that control your destiny are only there

because *you* let them be.

August 30. Something About It

We can't help but change

When we help what we change.

Change happens when you decide

It's no longer possible to ask someone else to do

something

You're not willing to do yourself.

August 31. Eventually

If you find it hard to be *true* to yourself,

It's true that *you* will eventually be hard to find.

September

September 1.   It's Your Fault

Love is always at fault,

Better to be guilty

All the time.

September 2.   Miracle Expectations

Never expect miracles. Just know they're out there.

September 3.   'A'

Always

Accentuate

Another's

Abilities

And

Above all,

Ask, assist, assure, and acknowledge.

September 4.   Aligning the Stars

If you are waiting for all the starts to align

And for everything to become fair in your life,

You have chosen a long line to wait in.

September 5.   Couldn't Think of It

Some say enthusiasm is the most important thing in life.

I couldn't think of a second thing.

September 6.   Don't Take It

When someone corrects or reprimands you,

It's easy to snap back at them.

Don't give that person any response.

Take nothing personally.

Tons of freedoms come from that. Just get to it—
letting go.

Don't let someone make you feel negative and
emotional. *Only* you can do that.

There are those who continually correct, scold, or
seemingly get after the entire world.

Only you control your emotions.

Never let someone else get under your skin.

Don't just take it; sometimes fake it.

September 7.   In Their Lives

People who don't want you in their lives,

Don't deserve you in theirs.

September 8.   Your Perspective

Your perspective, as they say,

Some people can't hear it without first seeing it,

While others can't see it without hearing it.

It's called auditory or visual.

The key to success in life is hearing what you see and
seeing what you hear—

A good way to describe how to see what you've heard
about success in life.

September 9.   It's Not That Tough

To get ahead in life, we need to change our minds slowly
and make decisions fast.

Money moves fast, but accumulating it is not that tough

If you simply spend less than you earn.

Life is always about learning and earning,

And it's not that tough.

September 10.　Who To Please

We could spend our whole lives trying to oil the squeaky
wheel.

But the wheel you should try to please in life is right atop
your own shoulders.

Get it?

It's you.

When you get right down to it, it's not about them.

It's about who?

You.

September 11.　Life's Business Plan

1. Start with knowing what you want.

2. Make a list based on your goals.

3. Review progress daily.

4. Never give up; never give in.

5. Have the conclusion you seek be something that
    either

    a) makes you financially more secure,

    b) helps others,

c) puts a smile on your face, or

d) is a no-fault, change-in-process program.

5. Once you complete life's business plan, move into the action phase until you reach the desired Accomplishments.

Without a life plan, your life will be unplanned.

September 12.   Heavy Lifting

When you weigh the results of *action*,

Inaction doesn't even move the scale.

September 13.   Direction Optional

Providing options instead of directions is what's called Optional.

People have the ability to solve their own problems. Don't get in their way; just go ahead and let them.

September 14.   One Leg at a Time

No matter how fast they tell you to run,

It is still done one leg at a time,

Unless you're a kangaroo.

September 15.   In *Deed*

A friend doing a good deed

Is a man paying it forward

In case he's ever in need.

September 16.   Appreciation

Appreciate what we do have more than we worry about

    what we don't have.

September 17.   Foolish

It's hard to fool a fool.

Why try? For if you do,

You become one too.

September 18.   Stay *Away*

Comfort zones are like

Guard rails on life's highway.

You need to

Keep your distance,

If your plan is to keep

Moving forward.

September 19.   What's in a Smile?

1) Sunshine

2) Happiness

3) Laughter

4) Acknowledgement

5) Understanding

6) Fun

7) Friendship

8) Joy

9) Peace

10) Acceptance

11) Fearlessness

12) Kindness

13) Hope

14) Love

15) Guidance

16) Family

17) Beginnings

18) Summer

19) Appreciation

20) Appeal

September 20.   The Joneses

Why keep up with them?

Why try to compete?

Why spend the energy?

It is not going to be easy to beat.

So when someone tries to copy you, don't see it as an
   insult.

Take it as a compliment of your skills and your good
   decisions.

That's how to keep up with it.

Be yourself—a much better solution.

September 21.   Quiet Please

Many a time, I've wished my words could return

To my mouth

Haven't you had that experience?

September 22.   *Whatcha* Missing?

More people should stop thinking about what they're
    missing and
Think more about what everyone else is missing.

September 23   Daily Dose

Morning vitamins consist mainly of *enthusiasm*.
Being *enthusiastic* has no age limits.

September 24.   Figure It *Out*

Resourcefulness means having the ability to deal with
    situations.
Dad always said, "Deal with it."

The greatest motivation of men and women usually
    comes from
You-know-who
In the form of a good kick in the
You-know-where.

September 25.   The Grudge Match Within

A wise old man once said, "Holding a grudge and
expecting it to change something or someone for you,
is like drinking poison and expecting the other person
or thing at fault to be sickened."

Get over it doesn't mean *forget it*, but it means release the
other person and stop holding grudges.

You will benefit by releasing the grudge match that's
within you.

September 26.   Doing It Justice

Most times, if you do what you say,
You won't be held to always saying what you do.
It's called the accountability experience.

When people know you're good for your word, they
leave it at that.

No more checking to see if you actually did what you said
    later.

That's why we say, "*Just* do it today."

September 27.   Keep Asking

We are able to answer many of life's questions.

Keep asking the questions out loud,

And answers will follow.

Neither Google nor Yahoo has the all the answers,

But you do.

September 28.   *Ouch!*

The *truth* is like hitting your finger with a hammer.

It seems to hurt more when someone else is holding the
    hammer's handle

And hitting *you*

With it.

September 29. Green Environment

Regardless of the environment you live in,

No one is going to hand you *success*.

Train yourself.

Read, write, practice, prepare,

And get busy being busy.

It's for you; it's not for the environment.

September 30. Just One Skill

Expand one key skill beyond normal, maybe approaching
exceptional.
Your life will change.

October

October 1.   Can You See It?

What you do determines what you'll see.

People don't know what it can be.

They only know what they see.

October 2.   A Doctor's Prescription

The *best* advice you can give yourself

Is that today and every day,

You are always improving in every way.

October 3.   *Good*

Good things come to those who believe.

Great things happen to those who take action.

Get busy and keep believing.

October 4.   Live Like Children

*L*ive

*I*n

*F*un

*E*very

*S*econd.

*A*lways

*B*ecome

*E*xcited,

*A*s

Children

*H*ave.

October 5.   Sergeant Schultz

Intelligence, to me,

Is knowing

I

Really

Know

Nothing.

October 6.   Hula-Hoop

When you feel like life has you jumping through hoops,

Consider this:

Maybe the world just knows you're good at Hula-Hoop.

Shake your booty.

October 7.   Are You Young?

Recent studies reveal,

As reported by today's mature adults,

Enthusiasm is what keeps them young.

October 8.   Someone Else's World

Make *more* sense.

Leave someone more *cents*

Don't live senselessly.

Use your common sense.

Never get caught up in senselessness.

Always operate with sensibleness.

October 9.   If You Ran Each Day

Get better in some way (each day).

Perk up the world (each day).

Make someone's life easier (each day).

Lift up someone who's down (each day).

Help develop the poor (each day).

Enhance the world (each day).

Expand someone's vision (each day).

Get better at looking up (each day).

Adjust your negative thinking (each day).

Touch someone positively (each day).

All of this is called polishing the world and the people in
it (each day).

October 10.   Questions

He who has *no* why

Lives without question.

He who knows how

Lives knowing why.

October 11.   Learning from You

What you tell yourself is far more important than what

anyone tries to tell you.

You can accomplish anything in life

If you direct your own actions toward

What *you've* been telling yourself all along.

October 12.   Hard Work or Hardly Working

There is a distinct parallel between wealth and work.

There is an even closer link between extremely hard work

and extremely high wealth.

Do you get it?

Hard work delivers wealth.

(Just *no* promises.)

However, statisticians would agree, the odds of

   accomplishment are weighted in your favor

When you work hard.

Now get going.

October 13.   Uplift Yourself

If you want to fly,

You've got to get both feet *off* the ground.

It's called life's dance.

October 14.   Know Nothing at *All*

I think I know that admitting we know very little is

Proof we are smarter than we think.

October 15.   Getting a Lifelong "A"

For a life filled with attainment, achievement, awards,

   accolades, and advancement,

What do you leave behind?

Can nots, could nots, would nots, should nots, did nots,

Might haves, would haves.

Instead, fill your day with lots of

Cheer and laughter, hope and praise,

Attempts and try-to's.

Just never give up.

October 16.   Keep on Keeping on

Perseverance does not mean a long race.

It is *many* short races,

One after another.

October 17. Edison and Others

What would the world be like without invention?

Great things have come from innovation.

Resistance to difference can cause persistent inconsistency.

Embracing change opens new worlds, new doors, and
new opportunities.

Greats like Edison, Ford, and Einstein kept on trying new
items to effect change for the better.

What results are possible for *you* when you pursue change?

Anything is possible.

October 18. Getting Busy

The person who achieves the most will always be the
most action-filled, positive-filled individual.

When you get into action, lots of walls drop, doors open,
opportunities arise, and you physically achieve.

So why not do it? You're the beneficiary.

October 19.   Simple Pleasures

Some of the *greatest* pleasures

Known to man have to do with

Doing what people say cannot be done.

October 20   Keep On Trying

If at first, *you* don't try,

You can't succeed.

Well then *you*, try, try again.

October 21.   Bigger than Life

I've had friends who were bigger than life.

Their *aura* of greatness shined through with blinding light.

I knew they were near before they'd appear.

But once they are gone I was lucky to just have seen

them here.

I love you my many friends, till we meet again, thanks for
being my friend.

October 22.   *Limits*, No Limits

Expertise lifts you *higher,*

Intelligence goes wherever it wants to.

October 23.   Possessions

What you have

Has little to do with enjoying your happiness.

October 24.   Never Have

Do the work others aren't willing to do,

And you'll get the things others will never have.

October 25.   The Circle of Life

Encircle your life with friends and family members who
   elevate you.
It's that simple.

Good things come to those who believe.
Great things happen to those who take action.

October 26.   Control *You*

Control how you think.

Control how you feel.

Control how you react.

Control how you speak.

Control how you see.

Control how you go.

Examining all these simple formulas has shown us that
   you control a lot.

So stay in control of yourself, not others.

You're good.

October 27.   Peace

We all find ourselves, from time to time, being collectors

of collections,

Also known as keepers of things.

Why is that?

Guess everyone has his or her own reasons.

Peace cannot be truly found simply by collecting pieces.

October 28.   The Alarm Clock

The only person to wake up today is that sleeping giant.

(It's you.)

Wake up; *no* one is going to do it for you.

No one.

October 29.   School Them

Teach your children the *right* way, early on,

So someone else doesn't try to teach the *wrong* way,

later on.

October 30. Something Worthy

How do you spell accomplishment?

It centers mainly around the M.I.T. principle,

Which says to complete something worthy, you must

   commit yourself to the tasks required.

Seems simple doesn't it?

October 31. Performance

Don't make

Predictions based

On your past performances

And

Failures.

Make them based on your faith in yourself.

November

November 1.   Whatever It Is

When it's time to let go of whatever it is that's holding

you back,

Just hang on a little while longer.

You've hung on this long to whatever it is.

The letting go should be the easy part.

Just think how hard it's been holding on to whatever it is.

November 2.   Simple, Isn't It?

It may seem smart to keep it simple,

But most times being too simple just isn't smart.

Education and learning are lifelong, never-ending tasks.

Education and learning forever isn't

A theory.

It's a practice.

November 3.   Confusion

A confused individual is in pursuit of knowledge of
   oneself.
Just in case you forgot, people will tell you a lie, *proving*
   their lies are their problem.

November 4.   Complications

Leading a complicated life?
Let others live without your complications—
Maintaining their complicated lives is how they avoid
   change.

The less you worry about what some people think, the
   less complicated your life becomes.

November 5.   Worrying

Worrying will never, ever change the outcome.
Whatever you are worrying about it is a total

Time waster.

People should know this, but they don't.

November 6.   Teachers Teach

If schools would continue to educate their teachers
using the same methods practiced on their students,
just what grades would the students give out to the
teachers?

Always thought the kids should be allowed to grade
the teachers, the same way the teachers grade their
students.

November 7.   Do You Get It?

You are a success
Once you have given up saying you are not.

November 8.   How Are Yours

Priorities straight up keep everything else in line.

It's important to examine yours from time to time,

To make sure that you have kept

Your own priorities present and accounted for.

Have you?

November 9.   How You Deal

Always try to be fair when dealing with people.

Seems so incredibly simple, but it can be so incredibly

   difficult.

Try it; you'll like it, and so will they.

November 10.   In or Out

Ordinary is out.

Extraordinary is in.

November 11.   Everything

What you give is what you get, right?

No—

You get much more when you give away what you have.

What you get? You get everything.

November 12.   It Usually Never Is

It's usually not good when it's too good to be true.

But let me ask you this,

Didn't you already know that?

November 13.   See It

A wise, blind man enjoys his knowledge

While never needing to see it to believe in it.

November 14.   Accomplishing Anything

To

Reach

A final goal,

No matter how fast

Or slow

You go,

(Most importantly)

Never stop

Or let it go.

November 15.   Stupid Is As

I know you're *not* ignorant.

Now just *stop* proving it.

November 16.   It Is There If You Listen

When *you* listen for silence, *you* get to enjoy the sounds.

November 17.   Get Back Up

Getting up isn't an option,

But if you are going to succeed,

You are going to keep falling down.

November 18.   Duck

No matter what life throws at you,

The simple fix is to make it simple and always be flexible
enough to duck.

November 19.   When Do You Make It?

If you don't buy it at the right price, you can't sell it at the
right price.

You make your money the day you buy something, not
the day you sell it.

November 20.   Excuses

Do people really make excuses for not being happy?

Today, make an excuse to be happy.

We'll excuse you for that.

November 21.   Stop Waiting

If you want results, take action.

If you won't take action,

You don't really want results.

Stop being corrupted by your own indecision.

November 22.   Change or Chance

When are you going to take a chance?

It's not necessary,

Unless you want change.

November 23.   Yes, You Can

Am I?

I am.

They said *you* couldn't do it.

They said *you* shouldn't try.

I guess they didn't know you, and that's the reason why

You'll never be known as a failure, just as long as, yes,

   you try.

Failure isn't final. Defeat doesn't mean you're beat.

Almost anything is possible—but first you've got to try.

Never give up.

I have faith in you.

November 24.   Fooled Again

If *you* can continue to fool yourself,

Do *you* think the rest of the world is just as gullible?

November 25.   Accept Life's Circumstances

Accept Life's Circumstances

Or embrace your role for making the difference.

Excuses deliver discouragement.

Actions ensure results.

November 26.   What Do You Know?

People's lifelong learning consists of very little.

What people need to search out isn't what they already
  know about,

But rather what they don't know about.

November 27.   Life's Account Balances

Friendships, like fortunes, require deposits

Before you can make withdrawals.

Balance your accounts and friends, being careful that you
  have excess in the friends ledger.

Thank you all for being my friends.

I appreciate you all.

November 28.   Finally Positive

The newspaper called the other day and asked for a
    quote.
The next day's headline read, "The News Media is
    Reporting Lots of Closings, but Some Delays."
Finally, positive news about the real estate market!

Wrong.
Simply another weather report.

Life's problems must be solved.
So do that one, scary thing first
Each day.

November 29.   The Right Delivery

Wrong never delivers right.

When it seems like life has delivered more wrong than
right, look around *you.*

It is easy to count your blessings and know there's always
far more right than wrong.

Be the person the

World wants to see.

The best way to calculate all the positives in our own lives
is to count our blessings.

November 30.   How Do You Consider You?

Those who hang on to a tiny hope may be holding on by
a thin thread.

December

December 1.   Listen Up

In sales and in life, it is not what you hear your clients and
friends saying that spurs the sale or the smile.
It is figuring out what they aren't saying that unlocks the
sale and the friendship.
If you can listen more than you talk, you are on your way.

It isn't what's said, it's what's unsaid.

December 2.   Natural Ability

Lacking the ability to look forward, toward forgiveness,
forces us backward into blame,
Where excuses keep us from the present.

December 3. To Be or Not to Be

Be an example, not an exception.

Take full responsibility for you. If *we* are to be, it's up to
  you and me.

That's why they call it *we*.

December 4. Put Them to Use

Use your

Abilities

Or they will become your

Disabilities.

December 5. Listen for It

The preacher said a lot,

But very little really got said.

The End.

Amen.

P.S. His congregation remarked, "Short and sweet. It was
one of his best."

December 6.   Magic Accomplishments

Good planning *never* ensures future success,
But it lays the foundation for failure to be a thing
Of the past.

Also called "accomplishment lists,"
Once put to paper, magic occurs.

When pen is in hand and words appear,
That changes everything near.

December 7.   Whose Policy Is It?

Life's return policy:
Yes it is important to love yourself,
But life's return policy is all about giving what you have
to another and to the world.

It's time to go back to the basics in life and practice your
show-and-tell policy.
Show and tell everyone how very much you love
them all.

It's shouldn't be a script or an act.

December 8.   Are You Blind?

Those who dislike work
Are blinded to the
Opportunities that stare
Them in the face.

December 9.   You Can

If you don't like your direction,
Maybe take direction from someone else.

December 10.   It's Your Move

When you live in the city called Limited City,

Your stuff will never get on the moving truck headed to a

    better location called

New Heights.

December 11.   You Think

Please don't tell me what you think,

Tell me only that which you know.

December 12.   Keep Going

What is left to give when you've given all you've got?

Whatever it is, just never give it up.

December 13.   The Symptoms of Results

Rarely.

Results in life rarely get accomplished by setting deadlines.

Funny how it seems to fit right there next to "I'll get to it
   later" and "make me a list."

Guess they haven't developed a drug that cures the
   symptoms of "Someday just yet."

December 14.   Your Voice

We're all given a vocal chord,

Let's *not* use it wrong and strike a chord.

Life's best answer is, many times, left *unsaid*.

It's the reverse of use it or lose it—

Don't use it or you might *lose* it.

December 15   Your Daily Treat

Treat everyone fairly.

Be kind and polite.

In business and in life, the best policy is not to prey on

people,

But to pray for people.

Amen.

December 16.   Silence

They say the quiet ones are the ones to watch.

I say who are *they*?

We actually learn the most from the people who say the

least.

Give yourself a quiet time out.

Knowledge comes from listening, rarely from talking.

Make today great by being your own best hearing aid.

December 17.   Do You Do This

Either

Stand

In

Faith

Or

Fall

For

Lack

Of

It.

December 18.   Unstable

For me, the earth seemed unsettled, wobbly, constantly
    shifting.
My entire search has been trying to find stable ground.
What are you searching for?
Whatever it is, don't expect it to be found on even ground.

December 19.   Keep Trying

Change what you can change,

The rest is someone else's problem.

December 20.   Be Known

Ask yourself each day one important question.

What's the right thing to do?

This goes to a big-picture, headline statement of life.

Integrity in action!

Not Integrity—*inaction.*

Always try to do the right thing. Be known by everyone

as that integrity-filled individual.

December 21.   Gathering Time

Give me an old-time reunion.

It's best when faith, hope, and sincerity all come together

and share some of their love with a

Heartwarming hug they call togetherness.

December 22.   Left or Right

Ask yourself,

People who've left you feeling sad and depressed or

angry should be just that.

Left, isn't that right?

When you feel like giving up, just chalk it up and say

instead, "I've had enough instead."

December 23. Faith—Yours

Those who lack faith in themselves will struggle to find
  any other faith.

If you can believe in yourself, you can find time to believe
  in many other things in life.

December 24. Comments

A friend of mine commented, "No way possible."

We say, "If you're going to *commit*, there's a way."

December 25. Help

Doing nothing and expecting something
Reminds us of one, unjust, wealthy person standing on
  the roadside, holding a cardboard that reads,
"Broke. Need money."

December 26.   Far Away

It's *okay* to shed a tear; it may be for those far and near.

Cherish the ones who've made your day, and always

remember the good times

When they're away.

December 27.   A Hello

Your future is calling you.

You have the power

Within you to change.

Are you going to answer?

December 28.   Maybe It's Just

When you can't hear what people are trying to tell you,

maybe it's just because you're not really listening.

Don't blame them.

Maybe they were trying to help and your ears were out of

order.

December 29.   Become Accountable

Accepting responsibility

Doesn't take

Action.

It takes accountability for

Inaction.

December 30.   Seeing It Change

What are the things you would like to see change in the
world?

The changes you wish to see don't necessarily need to
change the world.

December 31.   Hope

An optimist needs little hope.

The pessimist has little hope.

Don't give up hope; it's not the end.

Everything will be okay.

If it's not, it's just not the end.

Conclusion

I sincerely hope you've enjoyed *Enthusiasm Every Day*.

Reading a page a day is an affirmation itself, one that helps the reader acquire the necessary knowledge to keep him or her growing.

Review this book and its quotes periodically. If you find yourself up against a difficult situation, the answer is probably within its pages.

Whatever regular program of development you are currently involved with, I am sure these pages of wisdom and experience will be a great reference and inspirational resource.

I hope you enjoyed every page, benefitted from its information, and most importantly, learned to grow in your search for life's answers.

Growing and building your own mental strength is of utmost importance. Building upon *you* is never done. Finding *you* is a noble aspiration; your priorities in life are the impressions you leave upon the world. Always strive for greatness and self-fulfillment.

We wish you a safe and exciting journey as you achieve and soar to even greater heights.

Never, ever let yourself quit.

Author Recommendations

Excellent! Mark Gleason captures the lessons of life we have learned over our lifetime and delivers them to us in a daily format that allows us to digest each one every day! Everyone will benefit from Mark's Enthusiasm Every Day!

-Allan Domb

This is some good stuff. I like the concept and I can see how access to a simple, inspiring, new message each day can help motivate people and keep them on track. Definitely a valuable tool in the arsenal of personal development.

-Dr. Steve Taubman

Mark, for years I have been a staunch proponent of, "It's easier to act your way into a new way of thinking than to think your way into a new way of acting" and Enthusiasm Every Day is a definite KEY to ACTION and coach of your inner voice.

Mark Gleason has cleverly pined 365 days of inspiration aspirations, both internal and external, that will hold one to a course of positive success. Daily he'll take you from enlighten to enlightenment and give power to your personal Enthusiasm!

-Rossi Speaks

I am well known for having a very positive mental attitude and the main reason is that I purposefully choose my 30,000 – 60,000 daily thoughts. I do that by choosing to read positive, inspiring, and uplifting books like Mark Gleason's.

One of the things I noticed and loved the most about Mark's book is its originality and thought provoking content. I have read over 500 different development books and after that many, much of what I read is repetition.

I found so many new and original thoughts and phrases in Mark's book it was refreshing. Some of the daily sayings in Mark's book sound like the wisdom and quotes I have read by Dr. Seuss, which I love. Buy this book and read it every day. It will help direct your thoughts, which is crucial for your long-term happiness, success, and positive attitude.

-Tom "Too Tall" Cunningham